UNDER A HOLDERNESS SKY

Under a Holderness Sky

Norah Hanson

Valley Press

First published in 2013 by Valley Press
Woodend, The Crescent, Scarborough, YO11 2PW
www.valleypressuk.com

ISBN: 978-1-908853-33-2
Cat. no.: VP0051

A CIP record for this book is
available from the British Library

Printed and bound in Great Britain by
Volume Ltd, Reading, Berkshire

www.valleypressuk.com/authors/norahhanson

Contents

A Confusing Journey 9
My House 10
My Feet Take Me Where They Will 12
My Granddaughter Saw Angels 14
When the Music Played 15
White Woman Dreaming 16
I Hear It Sometimes 17
Mother 18
Balancing the Books 19
The Fruit Bowl 21
Angels Never Pee 23
The Stand Off 24
Loud We Are 26
Life Expectations 27
Too Soon It Is Over 29
Walking with Ghosts 31
The Taste of You 33
A Room for You 34
High Above the Earth 35
Leaving 36
Christmas Season, 2011 37
The Ancient Plant 40
The Leaving of You 41
Walking Away 42
Heart Leap Child 44
In the Post Office Queue 45
First Love 46
Day Dreaming 47
Ambition 48
Beverley Westwood, 2001 50
Days of Blossoming Hawthorn 52
In the Silence of Their Stopping 53
Before I Die 54
Grandma's Blessing 56
Under a Holderness Sky 57

to family, friends
and good companions
who have shared my journey

A Confusing Journey

Don't swat the butterfly
brushing against your skin.
It has no bite or sting.
Programmed to evolve;
from creeping caterpillar
to chrysalis, to flying beauty,
is a confusing journey.

Unused to the air beneath
its wings, it blunders a little,
mistaking your face for a flower.
Be blessed.

My House

My house is a topsy-turvy house. It has shifted,
sunk and settled. Coins, beads and marbles
roll downhill to skirting boards which provide entry
for mice to take up residence in cold winter months.
It has been struck by lightning; the chimneystack
demolished, windows imploded, energy travelled
down the aerial, exploded the television, toppled
bookshelves and earthed in a gas pipe.

Dry rot, lurking behind asbestos, spread tentacles.
Roof beams, ceilings, rafters and walls were bashed
down and rebuilt. Workmen lost half a brick, which
lodged in the drain and caused toilet waste to back
up and ooze through cracks in the concrete of my
back yard. I was sold double glazing which buckled
under the weight of brick arches. Doors painted
and repainted no longer shut properly.

I care for, bandage and repair my topsy-turvy house.
The outside is pink, the colour of roses in summer.
I paint light on inside walls, gather wild flowers
to stand in jam jars, hang crystals round light bulbs
and blu-tack children's paintings on cupboard doors.
The morning sun shines in my kitchen, the setting
sun is framed in my front room window. My house
smells of casserole, bread and constantly brewing tea.

My house and I creak and groan as we settle to sleep.
One day, when my remains are worm food, my house
may sigh, a long last sigh and give up the ghost.
Spiders will scuttle from broken webs, resident mice
will vacate the premises, birds will fly from eaves
and in the ruins someone may find shards of crystal
which once shone in the dancing light of morning
and reflected the glowing colours of the setting sun.

My Feet Take Me Where They Will

I lock the front door, open the garden gate,
and let my feet take me where they will.
I wonder where all the people and cars
are coming from and going to, where the
planes making white streaks in the sky are
flying from and to, while I, who scurried
between this place and that place, to do
this job or that job, to meet this person or
that person, now wonder where I will go.

My feet take me on a familiar route, through
streets I trekked as a child on quiet Sunday
afternoons when parents went to bed after
dinner and children huddled in doorways
to whisper smutty jokes. I had been to Mass
and couldn't join in for fear of mortal sin.

Shops were closed then and streets empty
of cars. A stray dog often walked with me,
before sniffing at a promising scent, yelping
a farewell and trotting off on a new adventure.

I would walk over Barmston Drain, where
the water was heated by the cooling tower
on the bank and boys, some in bare buff,
would dive into the drain, while mothers,
wearing pinnies and turbans after work
in Needlers sweet factory, sat outside their
front doors on warm summer evenings.

They would gossip and watch their lads
at play as they chewed on reject toffees.
We girls would hide behind the bridge
wall and squeal when a boy's little penis
wobbled and his bottom flashed white
between the tan of his legs and back.

Today, bankside houses and the cooling tower
are demolished. Naked young boys are staid
old men or dead. Lorries trundle on the road;
the drain is a tangle of algae, a rusty shopping
trolley sticks out of the water and dogs on leads
are yanked away from tempting scents.
I let my feet take me where they will.

My Granddaughter Saw Angels

My granddaughter saw angels in flight
when the sky darkened to slate blue
and rooftop aerials gleamed in sunlight.
'Look', she said, *'they've brought a rainbow.'*
I saw them; bright silver-winged arrows
swooping, darting, as the arc of the rainbow
deepened in colour and bands of red,
gold, pink, green, purple throbbed
radiance in a holy sky.

My eyes became clear as washed windows,
reflecting polished verdure of tree and grass,
freshly experienced reds of brick walls,
rain dropping diamonds through space
and all the while the winged messengers,
clothed in silver, dancing joy, flashing
against the dark translucence of the sky.

When the Music Played

When the music played and I was a child,
I could tumble into trickling notes,
become a ripple in sunlit water dancing over stones.
The flute could take me soaring beyond concrete streets
and grey poverty to fields, forests, lakes and lagoons
where sunset painted beauty over blue mountains.
I thought God spoke in the deep bass of the cello.

When the music played and I was a child,
she lay still on white satin cushions
inside a white box. She was dressed in a cream gown
with a silver star on her breast. They told me she was
sleeping with the angels. I thought she would wake up
when God spoke in the deep bass of the cello, and play
in fields as the sunset painted beauty over blue mountains.

When the music played and I was a child,
I did not hear the funeral dirge,
I did not see my mother's tears.

White Woman Dreaming

It is enough now to be still by
the fire, sheltered from winter.

I have ridden the train home
as the western sky painted
green lagoons and oceans
under blue mountains.

White woman dreaming;
fragrance of eucalyptus,
people smiling in the sun,
ancient black man's music
reverberating anthems.

I have leaned into the wind,
figurehead on a boat leaping
through warm waters, cried
out to whales flashing electric
blue as they raced to breed
in diamond seas. I have swam
where fish played in coral reefs.

Jets have winged me across
continents, brought me through
rain canopy to tarmac, moving
belts, fatigue and rail stations.

It is enough now to be still by
the fire, sheltered from winter.

I Hear It Sometimes

I long to hear the song I once knew,
lost in discords of experience;
an intrusive cacophony, thundering,
beating, dimming the faint echo
of half-remembered music.

I hear it faintly when the wind blows
through chattering leaves, when
vapour rises from the early morning
garden, and in the silence of night.
A haunting melody of distant pipes,
calling me forward to my past.

Mother

I can feel her drawing closer and wonder why.
Every day the retelling of her memories overlays
the events of my life. Her words echo in my head.
'It will pass, things always pass. Let it be for now.'
I think of the Beatles song. She knew the words
before it was written.

They have passed; my lover, parents and friends.
I thought it would be you, as it always has been you,
who would permeate my days, but it is she who is
the dominant gentle force these last few months.
I feel her strength, the comfort of her presence
and wonder why.

Balancing the Books

My mother told me to think
of the starving black babies in
Africa and eat up my sprouts.

I ate them all up, believing my
bloated belly and windy emissions
were penance for my sin of
ungratefulness and God would
forgive me and let the babies
have enough food and stop dying.
I saved my pennies to buy pictures
of black babies and prayed the
prayer on the back, asking their
guardian angels to watch over them.

'Count your blessings', she'd say
to me when she couldn't mend
the broken trivia of my life.
Do the accounts, list the debits
and credits, the kicks in the teeth
against the good times, and she'd
remember the good times for me
until the books balanced and
I stopped complaining.

Later, when tragedy came,
she told me: 'Everything passes.
Good times will come again.
We will balance the books
and count our blessings.
You will stop crying'.

Now her voice is silenced,
I still eat up my sprouts
and count my blessings.
I try to balance the books
but I've given up bargaining

Babies still starve to death.
Children die in wars. Some who
survive grow up to kill each other
in the name of their God.
Others escape massacre and torture,
and find their way to my country.
I sometimes cook them dinners.
They eat up their sprouts, pardon
themselves for windy emissions
and pray for me in the words
of the lost faith of my childhood.

The Fruit Bowl

My mother didn't have a fruit bowl.
There was no still life in our house,
no perfect polished fruit in a dish.
The greengrocer sold gammy apples
and pears for a penny a handful.
Mam cut away the bruised bits.
We devoured the fleshy succulence,
crunching our way to the cores,
nibbling round the pips.

Oranges were a Christmas treat.
The sharp tang, clean and crisp
on the smell of winter indoors.
Our top teeth scraped the pith,
juice dribbled down our chins
to sting our cold sores.
Dates and figs in boxes were bought
by posh people; we knew none.
We watched Tarzan and monkeys
eat bananas at Saturday matinees.

When I was seven, having reached
the age of reason, I fell in with bad
company, went scrumping in an
orchard, picked and held a ripe
sun-kissed pear in my hands, touched
the skin to my lips, salivated, dropped it
and ran when the farmer yelled.

It was my first real temptation; a sin
meriting an Our Father, three Hail Marys
and a Glory Be in confession. I would have
recited the entire mysteries of the Rosary
and the Salve Regina to have tasted that pear.

I now have a cut glass fruit bowl, filled with
shiny fruits picked from supermarket shelves.
I paint still life pictures of my fruit bowl
and crave the tastes of yesterday,
the forbidden fruit of my childhood.

Angels Never Pee

Sharing a bed, jostling for space,
burrowing into a feather mattress,
one sister's leg on another's waist,
her leg on my thigh, arms cuddling,
our breath incense in the cold air,
we thought our guardian angels
hovered in the shifting shadows
as the light faded from the window.
We thought we were safe.

Our little sister tried to make room
for her angel to sleep in our bed.
We told her there was no room
and her angel wouldn't like the
damp sheets when she peed
in the night. Angels never pee.
They don't need food, drink or sleep,
but she could sing to her angel,
just for a bit. Angels like music.

When our little sister died, the nuns
told us God had taken her to be an
angel in heaven. She wouldn't pee
in the bed again. Angels never pee.
Our bed was cold without her.
Sometimes, before I fell asleep,
I heard a sound, clear and beautiful
as marble ringing in the silence.
I thought she might be singing to me.

The Stand Off

Icicle spears hung from gutters, doors and archways.
The coalhouse was empty, the outside tap frozen.
Mam made a fire from sulphurous clinkers; gleanings
from the coal yard at the bottom of the street, fetched
in an old pram, they belched smoke and made us cough.

Wearing gloves, hat, scarf and two jumpers, I was
on watch in the cold front room, peering out from
the frosted window, for the randy coalman who
ignored our need for heat after our mam refused
him favours in return for a bag of good coal.

From my sore throat, I rasped, 'He's coming Mam'
as the cart, stacked with sacks of coal, made fast
progress up the street, the clack of the horse's
shoes muffled on packed snow, steam rising from
its hide as the randy coalman urged it on.

Mam charged out of the house, stood arms akimbo
in front of the startled horse which snorted hot
breath in her face. A stand off, as curtains twitched
and women in turbans and pinnies came onto the
street. He chewed his lower lip, spat into the snow.

The whites of his eyes showed wide against the
black dust coating his face. He dropped from
the cart, hefted a sack of fuel onto his back
and trudged to our back yard to tip out shiny
lumps of good black coal onto our clinkers.

Mam paid him an exact price, scooped up a scuttle-full to feed the fire and make it roar up the chimney-back. We sat, me and my brave mam, toasting bread on a long-handled fork, eating our fill and letting yellow butter dribble down our chins.

Loud We Are

Altogether at family funerals,
we meet afterwards to feast
and remember the good times.
Death brings out the best in us,
infuses us with life and energy.
Laughter is loud, music frantic;
skittle boards, banjos, guitars,
tin whistles and drums.

We sing at our festive funerals,
bodies pulsing blood, red cheeks
and whiskey-bright eyes.
Loud we are, drowning
the cavernous call echoing
out of the death chamber
deep beneath the earth.

Life Expectations

I expect trouble to come my way
and prepare by indulging in fearful
anticipations, my insurance cover
against the worst that can happen.
My expectations have been exceeded.

Death no longer takes me by surprise.
I am now a regular funeral-goer.
Age UK, who are expecting my death,
mail me price lists for a decent burial
I can pay for now and avoid inflation.

I wonder if they will measure me up,
allow for shrinkage of my ageing bones
and place my coffin in storage with
a sell-by date should I survive
their expected date of departure.

I expect to have morbid musings as I age.
I may become moribund like my Aunt Vera
who lay on her death bed for a whole month.
She surprised us all just before she died,
by calling out for Robert.

'Who the hell is Robert?' we asked.
Her husband Tom had died years ago
but it was Robert she called for before
taking her last breath.
Nobody expected that.

I expect to stop using dye on my hair soon.
I expect people will think me wiser when
I am white-haired, though I expect some
will disregard me or patronise me.
I expect my language will surprise them.

I expect young men who carry my suitcase
up steps from the underground will
continue to be surprised at the weight,
say 'No trouble' and make a quick getaway
before the next flight of stairs to King's Cross.

I expect the day will come when my kids
will suggest I am too old to travel on
my own and should consider selling up
and moving in with one or other of them.
I expect them not to succeed.

I expect the sun will rise each morning
whether I am here to see it or not.
I would like to be around in some form
or another, maybe in the in the air my
children breathe. I can't expect that –

but I can hope.

Too Soon It Is Over

We built a nest and sheltered our chicks,
foraged food from a teaching salary,
preened ourselves in clothes from
jumble sales and hand-me-downs.

Tender our sleep, your body holding mine.
A child wet wailing in the night, comforted
in our bed, we curled up in a moist tangle
of warm limbs until morning was heralded
before bird song by thumping feet and
piping voices marvelling at frosted artwork
on the inside of windows and our nostrils
filled with the freshness of winter indoors.
We put lighted candles in tins to stop pipes
freezing and left a week's supply of meat
in the refrigerated front porch.

Rosy-cheeked children round our table.
Shillings in the gas meter, milk porridge
cooked on the oven top. The kitten
squatting, shivering, leaving a yellow
heap on the floor. The door forced
open against drifted snow, which
slithered into my shoes, chilling my
unsocked feet as I carried a steaming
offering to the dustbin.

And the tumble and rush of days filled
with nappies, washing, cooking, picking
up Lego, children's prattle, stilled when
evening came. You sat at the table

marking books, I sewed buttons onto
shirts and darned socks until you came
to me with tea, red lips and suggestions.

Fleeting our time; they grew, we aged.
Too soon my love, too soon it is over.
You lie now in frozen earth, candles
in tins can't warm you. I grow old
in a centrally-heated house and miss
the winter days when coal fires roared
in chimney-backs, our blood ran warm
and rosy-cheeked children sat at our table.

Walking with Ghosts

They are with me always.
I shop for floor covering and wander
past the store, lost in conversation
with Aunty Pat who lived on this road
with a devil of a husband
whose smile could melt hearts.

She reared eight children, outlived
her husband by twenty years, watched
five of her children die and lived another
ten years before following them.

I tell her how I'd loved meeting her
on World Cup Final day in 1966,
when we'd dashed out during extra time
to buy weekend meat and she'd shoved
silver coins under the blanket of my pram
and told me my three bright-eyed boys
reminded her of her own babies.

The football scores were shouted
from shop to shop and she'd danced
a jig with the butcher when England won
and he'd planted a kiss on her lips.

My mother interrupts my musings,
telling me to make sure I take samples
home before I lay out money and I obey,
child again to the mother who would
have been a century old this year.

Back home, I wonder what you would think
and engage you in debate, enjoy arguing
for the hell of it as I did in days gone by.

We decide on a compromise and I ring the store
and pay by card, debiting the account which
used to be in both our names.

The Taste of You

In the lap of the village church,
this hide-and-seek playground
of your boyhood, deep down in
Wolds clay, limbs, torso, head,
all my hands caressed lies dead.

Roots of ancient trees tilt tombstones.
Rich compost grows juicy brambles.
I pick and taste the sweetness of you,
speak into the silence of your absence
and hear words echoing in the space
where energy danced between us.

A Room for You

When sleep takes me through doors I have locked,
to dry rot, mice droppings and moth-eaten linen,
I try to prepare a room for you to come home to.
I can't find clean sheets, dustpan or brush.
The floor boards break under my feet

and I fall and I fall into that sudden awakening
and a thirst on me for ice-cold water.
The resounding thrum of your absence
drives me from my bed to stand at the window
and watch the garden grow out of moon-dust.

There was such a light the night I lay with you
in the field when the white owl floated over us.
I will leave my bed tonight, lock the door on
rooms full of your absence and find you again
in the garden, growing out of moon-dust.

High Above the Earth

High above the earth, constellations diamond-
bright shone on the deep blue velvet of the night.
Wispy pale-green tails floated to the rim of the
world, as the aurora borealis gleamed in the north.

I thought of you swallowing medication before
sleeping in your lonely bed, curtains closed,
doors locked, lights switched off, content with
the concrete existence of order and routine.

You had scorned sleep to camp out on cold nights,
your head outside the flap of your tent watching
shooting stars, satellites and a haloed crescent moon.
You had strummed your guitar as the sky reddened
in the west and bird song greeted the dawn.

You had run naked into the North Sea as the clocks
struck midnight and an old year ended, shouting
your joy as bells pealed, ship's hooters blared,
fireworks exploded and your life promised good.
Beautiful you were, under the stars of winter.

High above the earth, I grieved the loss of your
brilliant spirit which dared too much, flew too
far and fell wounded into my arms.

POETRY LIBRARY

Leaving

She laid her heart between each folded shirt,
placed her hopes in the pockets of his vests.
She put her dreams into the arms of his sweaters,
her trust in the layers of his neatly folded linen.

She closed his suitcase and walked with him
to the station. Her hand brushed his arm.
Her farewell was brief and tearless.
As his train pulled away, he watched
her back as she walked away from his life.

Christmas Season, 2011

A robotic voice orders me to remove
unexpected items from the bagging area.
People in the queue behind me glower.
An official hurries to the 'fast track' lane
and impatiently explains that I am trying
to scan my shopping from right to left
instead of the other way round and I've
caused the machine to break down.

Sighing heavily, she escorts me to a queue,
where eventually, my shopping is scanned
by a weary till operator who insists I am
helped with my packing. The glowering
people are still waiting behind me.

Unfriendly mutterings follow me as I slink
through the sliding doors and take the
escalator down to the car park before
I remember I came in on the bus.

I wait fifteen minutes, flash my Senior
Citizen bus pass at the driver, who tells
me the procedure now is to place my pass
on the new scanner. Nervously I do so.
He flips my pass the other way round,
orders me to collect my ticket and quickly
reverses out of the station as I stagger
down the bus and hold tight to a pole.
The handles of my plastic carriers bite
into my wrists. Passengers comfortably
ensconced don't think me senile enough
to be offered a seat. I really need to pee.

Home, I drop my shopping onto the floor
and race to the loo. My heartfelt 'Glory be
to God' is heard by my neighbour who rings
the doorbell, thinking she heard me scream.

After a cup of tea and a chocolate biscuit,
I tackle the annual ritual of decorating the tree
which is fixed on its base in the front room.
I watch *Neighbours* and *Midsomer Murders*
as I festoon the greenery with baubles, tinsel
and paper flowers, bought from a gypsy lady
who sells me lucky charms, pegs, nail brushes
and tea towels. She calls less frequently since
I stopped smoking and she can't scrounge a fag,
but I have supplies for a lifetime. Standing
on a stool, I fix the silver star on the top branch,
unravel the lights, drape them on the tree,
switch on, and am surprised when they work.

When the phone rings, I turn round to answer it.
That's when the whole bloody thing sways, totters
and fells itself. I crawl from under it, wearing
a necklace of coloured lights, pine cones
and pointed leaves stuck in my clothes,
the silver star wobbling in front of my eyes,
its stick having parted my hair. I am
an illuminated hedgehog.

'*Good afternoon*', says the caller. '*Could you spare a few minutes to answer questions for a Government survey collecting data on the wellbeing of the nation, and what makes people happy? We are contacting a cross section of the populace and believe you are a widow living alone. Do you find Christmas stressful?*'

The Ancient Plant

With a pruning and a spraying
and a shaving and a snipping
and a nipping and a wrapping,
and a feeding and a watering,
the old plant survives the winter.

Spring comes, young shoots jostle
for space. Greedy for sunlight,
twining, pushing, creeping,
they thrust down eager roots,
spider-thin and tenacious,

birth fresh green leaves, wave
triumphant flower heads over
the ancient plant which shrinks
in the shade of their glory
as they bask in the sun's warmth.

The Leaving of You

The plane climbs into blue skies.
I watch the sea lapping the shore
where you take your sons to play.
The coastline trails like a ribbon
round the land you now call home.

Yesterday, I walked with you on
white sands in a dreamtime of
silent farewells, filling the space
between us with the missing of you.

You did not linger at the airport.
I did not look back at your going.

Today, the plane drops through clouds.
I trundle luggage to the interchange,
shiver on a steel bench, my sandaled
feet are cold on a slippery floor.
Fog sits in my jet-lagged brain
as the coach takes me north.

You are sleeping now; my morning
sun has sunk over your horizon.
I have moved into your past.
The space between us is filled
with the missing of you,
the leaving of you.

Walking Away

Holding hands, two children walk to
where the sea washes their feet.
They look at each other, look north,
look at their feet, then move as if
listening to music only they can hear;
their going uninterrupted when they
lower their heads to watch how
the wet sand separates their toes.
Briefly visible, their footprints
licked smooth by rippling waves.

The breeze blows warm on their backs,
lifts and caresses wisps of fine hair.
The sun above their heads seems to
pause on its westward path.

Lying on hot sand, the woman drifts
into a long-forgetful moment where
sound is a receding echo playing on
the murmur of the tide, and children
are shadows in the passing of her life.

Waking to throbbing radiance, she
stumbles to her feet, shields her eyes,
calls their names. Her voice is snatched
by screeching gulls riding thermals
breathed from the sighing summer tide.

Someone points to two haloed heads,
small figures disappearing into light haze.
She calls again, a fearful urgent cry.

The children stop, look at each other,
look at their feet, look back,
walk away.

Heart Leap Child

Newly born, your head resting in my hand,
your body still in my arms, your eyes were
dark pools of light. You listened when I spoke.
'Hello lovely. Have you come to live with us?'

As if waking from a deep sleep, you yawned,
stretched arms and legs, arched your back,
settled again in the cradle I made for you.
I was gaze-caught in the wonder of your eyes.
A shaft of love flashed in the space between us.
My heart leapt in response to your silent greeting.

In the Post Office Queue

They were a cheerful bunch of regulars
waiting to receive their benefits.
Greeted by the counter assistants,
they gossiped and confided.
The young child feasted on crisps
tipped onto the apron front of the buggy
which his mother pushed into a corner
while she chatted to her companions.

A stranger joined the queue, white hair
permed, cream dress freshly laundered
and her breathing was an unbidden sigh,
like the whimper of a dreaming dog.

The child's wordless voice objected
to the view of a wall filled with posters.
His mother swivelled the buggy.
He quietened, ate a crisp and stared.

Caught in his gaze, she looked away,
but he called her back, his cry a command,
her response a whimper.

Holding a soggy crisp, he watched her
until his eyes filled with tears
and he bawled out her distress.

First Love

The teacher was out of the room
when he kissed her.
She had no memories of kisses
bestowed so gratuitously,
though in her infancy, before
the orphanage, she thought
they must have been given.

In her best handwriting,
she wrote him a love letter.
After school she saw him
swinging in the playground,
his eyes excited, bony knees
braced to keep his balance.

She waved to him and he waved
her letter triumphantly,
while his friends sniggered
and her heart broke.

Day Dreaming

The child's eyes, wide with wonder,
stared at nothing I could see.
He looked into the space of angels.
I couldn't call him back until he bade
them farewell and chose to return.

He dreams less often now, as we all do.
I wish him quiet moments in his days
to recall the wonder he once knew
and see again the fields of heaven,
bright with light and calm with sound.

Ambition

'We can climb down here', he said.
I followed to a sheltered gully
in the cliff at Flamborough Head.
A lone gull perching on a rock
blinked one eye and ignored us.
The sea lapped lazily, breathing
gently as a sleeping giant.
The wind was a warm caress.
He had not climbed cliffs before.
The long white beaches of his
own land were approached
by inclines.

He said he was looking at
the North Sea, pointed to his left
and told me that was the direction
of the Arctic and the North Pole.
'Polar Bears live there', he said.
He was anxious about the melting
ice caps, the effect on the environment,
people who drop litter, cruel people,
who take lives, the homeless
and poor children who have no food.

I felt the weight of his worry, and told
him of people who work to make
the world a better place; how slavery
became unacceptable; how good
people speak up for the poor
and raise money for bore holes

and seeds; how scientists work
to find cures for illness; how things
can be mended and made whole,
of the beauty of music and art.

He sat awhile and then said:
'This place is so peaceful.
I could stay here forever'.
We stayed an hour.
He sang me an aboriginal song.
I heard an ancient anthem,
reverberating cry of creation,
in wind, ocean, bird song, bees,
the triumphant beat of existence.

We heard them calling us and began
our climb back. Before we reached
the top, he paused to look at the gull,
the horizon and the distant north
where the polar bears live.

'I will make the world a better place',
he said.

Beverley Westwood, 2001

(The year of foot-and-mouth disease.)

The Westwood is not grazed this year.
The common is a glorious meadowland
of buttercups, clovers and tall grasses
tinged with pink, waving seed heads
in the hot breeze of early July.

I had walked through the woods,
climbed the hill to the old mill.
Sweating and breathless, I rested,
wanting to take off my bra, tie it
round my straw hat, run down
the hill, across the golf course
and cause grey heads searching
for lost golf balls to look askance.
Sick with my lot, weary and alone,
I resented their contentment.

Sighing in the silence, I heard the wind
and the responding chatter of leaves
in ancient trees, watched grasses sway
to the rhythm of a song my life had lost.
I remembered the music which played
in the breeze when the child I once was
danced in the early-morning garden.

Sudden the squall, roar of thunder,
and weeping rage flattening the grass,
bowing the branches, bucketing a deluge
on me before the black cloud raced north.

I watched steam rise from the meadow
and heard, faint as a sigh from the edge
of eternity, the Westwood wind sing again.

Days of Blossoming Hawthorn

Wilting carnations in buttonholes, boozed up and raucous
young bucks in crumpled suits are lulled into drunken stupors
as the rhythm of wheels on tracks repeats. Pelmets of cloud
hang over power stations on the horizon. The sky is silver-lit
above pastures. Cattle are unfazed by the rush of our passing.
The girl with a flower in her dark hair smiles at her lover.

Tractors and diggers lie idle in fields where earth has been
scooped and levelled for house building. We race across
a canal, past hedgerows where hawthorn is white-blossoming,
gorse golden and horse chestnuts sport candelabra.
Old men tend allotments. A wind turbine rests in the still air.
Another canal, straight, glassy and gorgeous.

Sheep follow a leader through a gap in a hedge. A reflected
strip of carriage light keeps pace as we race through Gilberdyke.
Our twelve-seater bus died there many years ago. The girl with
the flower in her hair is asleep in her lover's arms. I have lived
her lifetime three times over. I remember your hand in mine.
My hands are blue-veined now and my fingers are arthritic.

My young skin could make you shudder with desire. I cannot
   bloom
again like the white hawthorn, nor can I sleep in my lover's arms.
Watchful of each passing moment, withering and heavy with
   memory,
I am being raced to my journey's end. Will you be there to meet me?
Or are you in my past, like the silver-lit fields of our youth, and
   the day
I wore a flower in my hair and smiled at your need for me.

In the Silence of Their Stopping

No need to hurry through the meadow
where tall grasses wave seed heads
and droning bees harvest wild flowers.
Time to stop and listen to bird calls
and the sighing of the summer breeze.

I am damp with sweat, freckles grow
on my arms. I smell my baking flesh,
take off my shoes, feel my calves caressed,
my toes and heels tingle-touched where
grass roots thrust from the earth.
Heat rises up my skirt, pinking my thighs.

High above the old town, the church spires
shimmer in the heat. I hear the distant peal
of bells and in the silence of their stopping
I think I hear your voice speaking my name.
And all the ages gone, to come, stop now,
in a present echoing eternity as I hear
again your voice speaking my name.

Before I Die

I will travel to Africa to see
elephants in the wild.
I will sit in a boat and paddle
the Okavango Swamps.
I will watch zebras galloping,
gazelles leaping, buffalos
bellowing over brown tundra,
flamingos pink in the sunset
landing, tip-tapping on water.

I will swat away the fly crawling on
the face of the child, let guides
cheat me of my money and not
listen to those who tell me it is
dangerous to travel alone.

I will stand on the Great Wall of China
to be a speck seen from outer space.
I will buy souvenirs from smiling
market traders in shanty towns
and let them cheat me of my money.

I will speak to the Aboriginal, painted
and feathered, playing his didgeridoo
for the tourists. I will smoke a cigarette
with him high up in the Blue Mountains
where the air smells of eucalyptus
and the people smile into the sun.

I will rest awhile then go north and
further north, to skies of ice blue,
where the shiver of winds disturbs
lakes and eagles nest. I will stand
in dark starlit nights and wait
for heaven to show me its gateway
descending, green gold and pink
flaming to the rim of the earth.

Grandma's Blessing

Health in the springtime of your life.
The hue of briar rose upon your cheek.
Strong and supple limbs to stride through
life and embrace all that it will offer.
Deep peace in your soul.
The courage of lions in your heart.

Love to fall like April rain on your hurts.
Love to shine like summer sun on your joys.
Love to gold-balm your sorrows
when September sunsets come.
Love in all your winter grieving
till new life wakes again.

Under a Holderness Sky

The heat of the sun lifts water from pavements.
Steam rises, returning rain to piebald clouds.
The wheels of my car hiss through roadside ponds.
Wings of silver spray arch and fall. I am flying
under the vast Holderness sky, racing to the coast,
chasing grey clouds and banks of snow-white
mountains, above the sun-bright blue brilliance
and the shimmering glory of a double rainbow.